GREAT SONGS
FOR GUITAR
CHORD SONGBOOK
THE BLACK BOOK

GW00801751

WISE PUBLICATIONS
part of The Music Sales Group
London/New York/Paris/Sydney/Copenhagen/Berlin/Madrid/Hong Kong/Tokyo

Published by
Wise Publications
14-15 Berners Street, London W1T 3LJ, UK.

Exclusive Distributors:

Music Sales Limited
Distribution Centre, Newmarket Road,
Bury St Edmunds, Suffolk IP33 3YB, UK.

Music Sales Pty Limited
20 Resolution Drive, Caringbah,
NSW 2229, Australia.

Order No. AM1004102
ISBN: 978-1-78038-375-0
This book © Copyright 2011 Wise Publications,
a division of Music Sales Limited.

Edited by Adrian Hopkins.
Produced by shedwork.com

Printed in the EU.

Your Guarantee of Quality:

As publishers, we strive to produce every book
to the highest commercial standards.

This book has been carefully designed
to minimise awkward page turns and to
make playing from it a real pleasure.

Particular care has been given to specifying
acid-free, neutral-sized paper made from pulps which
have not been elemental chlorine bleached.
This pulp is from farmed sustainable forests and
was produced with special regard for the environment.

Throughout, the printing and binding have
been planned to ensure a sturdy, attractive publication
which should give years of enjoyment.

If your copy fails to meet our high standards,
please inform us and we will gladly replace it.

www.musicsales.com

Ain't Misbehavin'

Words by Andy Razaf
Music by Thomas 'Fats' Waller & Harry Brooks

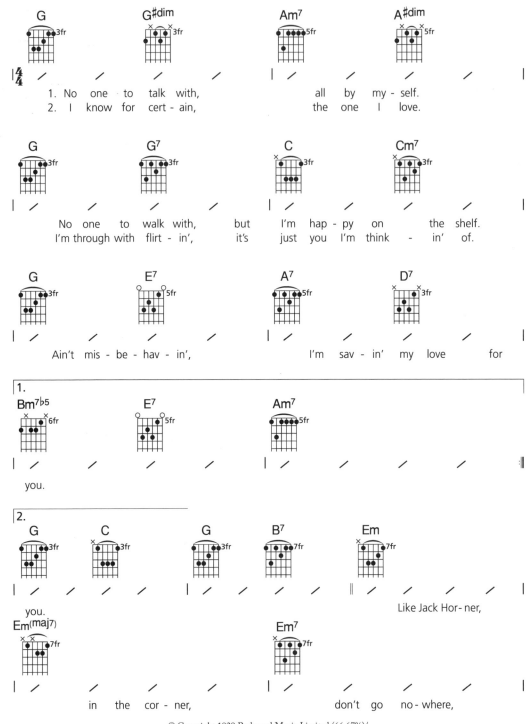

1. No one to talk with, all by my-self.
2. I know for cert-ain, the one I love.

No one to walk with, but I'm hap-py on the shelf.
I'm through with flirt-in', it's just you I'm think - in' of.

Ain't mis-be-hav-in', I'm sav-in' my love for

1.

you.

2.

you.

Like Jack Hor-ner,

in the cor-ner, don't go no-where,

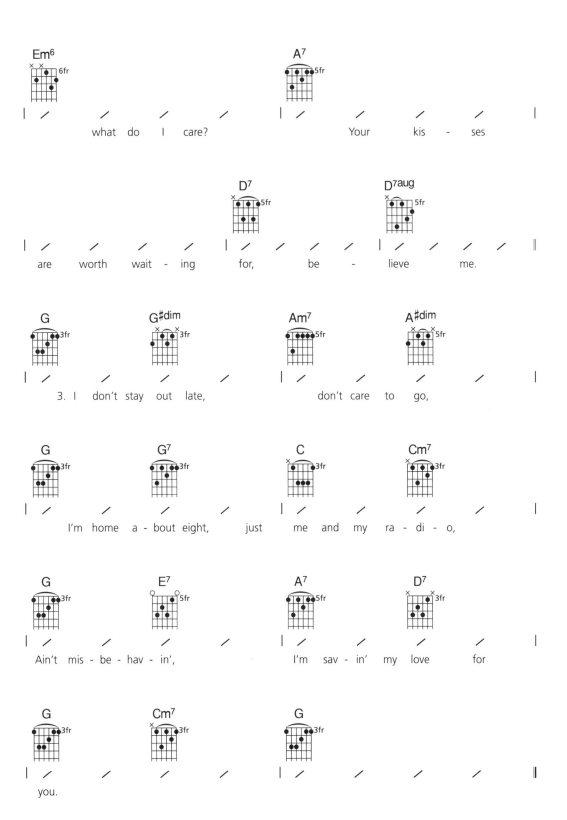

Em⁶

A⁷

| / | / | / | / | | / | / | / | / | |

what do I care?   Your   kis - ses

D⁷

D⁷aug

| / | / | / | / | | / | / | / | / | | / | / | / | / | ‖

are   worth   wait - ing   for,   be -   lieve   me.

G

G#dim

Am⁷

A#dim

| / | / | / | / | | / | / | / | / | |

3. I don't stay out late,   don't care to   go,

G

G⁷

C

Cm⁷

| / | / | / | / | | / | / | / | / | |

I'm home a - bout eight,   just   me and my ra - di - o,

G

E⁷

A⁷

D⁷

| / | / | / | / | | / | / | / | / | |

Ain't mis - be - hav - in',   I'm sav - in' my love   for

G

Cm⁷

G

| / | / | / | / | | / | / | / | / | ‖

you.

American Pie

Words & Music by Don McLean

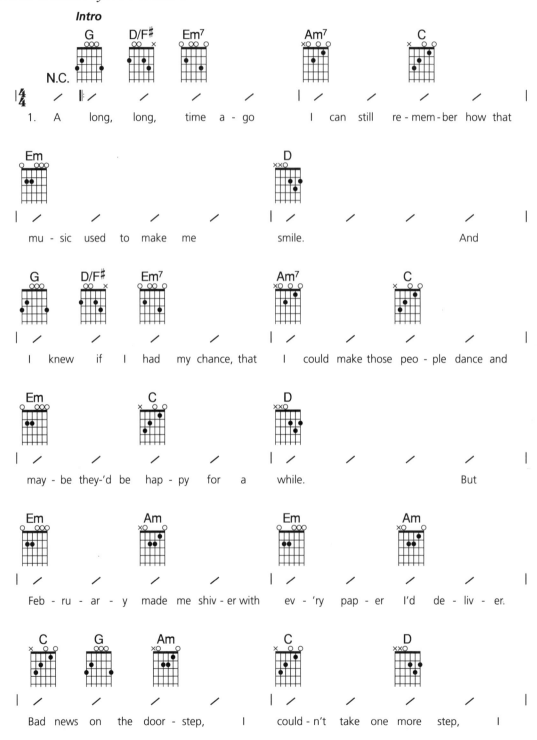

1. A long, long, time a-go I can still re-mem-ber how that

mu-sic used to make me smile. And

I knew if I had my chance, that I could make those peo-ple dance and

may-be they'd be hap-py for a while. But

Feb-ru-ar-y made me shiv-er with ev-'ry pap-er I'd de-liv-er.

Bad news on the door-step, I could-n't take one more step, I

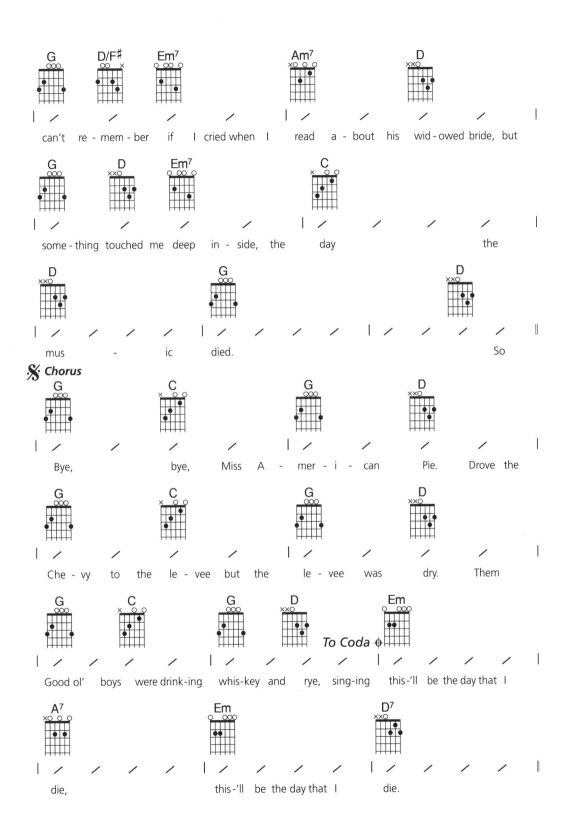

G   D/F#   Em⁷   Am⁷   D

can't re-mem-ber if I cried when I read a-bout his wid-owed bride, but

G   D   Em⁷   C

some-thing touched me deep in-side, the day the

D   G   D

mus - ic died. So

𝄋 Chorus

G   C   G   D

Bye, bye, Miss A - mer-i-can Pie. Drove the

G   C   G   D

Che-vy to the le-vee but the le-vee was dry. Them

G   C   G   D   Em

To Coda ⊕

Good ol' boys were drink-ing whis-key and rye, sing-ing this-'ll be the day that I

A⁷   Em   D⁷

die, this-'ll be the day that I die.

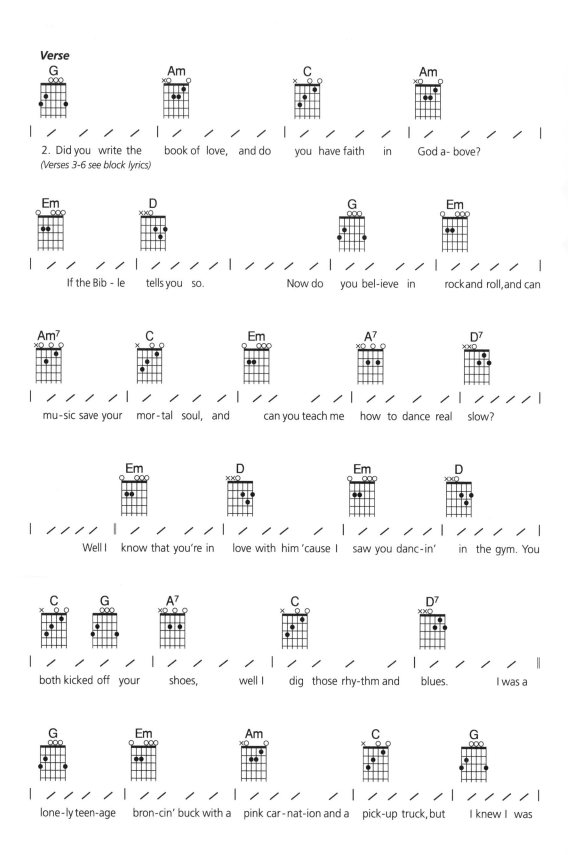

Verse

G   Am   C   Am

| / / / / | / / / / | / / / / | / / / / |

2. Did you write the   book of love, and do   you have faith   in   God a- bove?
(Verses 3-6 see block lyrics)

Em   D   G   Em

| / / / / | / / / / | / / / / | / / / / | / / / / |

If the Bib - le   tells you so.   Now do   you bel-ieve in   rock and roll, and can

Am⁷   C   Em   A⁷   D⁷

| / / / / | / / / / | / / / / | / / / / | / / / / |

mu-sic save your   mor-tal soul, and   can you teach me   how to dance real   slow?

Em   D   Em   D

| / / / / ‖ / / / / | / / / / | / / / / | / / / / |

Well I   know that you're in   love with him 'cause I   saw you danc-in'   in the gym. You

C   G   A⁷   C   D⁷

| / / / / | / / / / | / / / / | / / / / ‖

both kicked off your   shoes,   well I   dig those rhy-thm and   blues.   I was a

G   Em   Am   C   G

| / / / / | / / / / | / / / / | / / / / | / / / / |

lone-ly teen-age   bron-cin' buck with a   pink car-nat-ion and a   pick-up truck, but   I knew I was

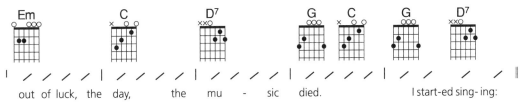

out of luck, the day, the mu - sic died. I start-ed sing-ing:

Chorus

Verse 3
Now for ten years we've been on our own,
And moss grows fat on a rollin' stone
But that's not how it used to be.
When the jester sang for the King and Queen
In a coat he borrowed from James Dean
And a voice that came from you and me.
Oh and while the King was looking down,
The jester stole his thorny crown.
The courtroom was adjourned,
No verdict was returned.
And while Lenin read a book on Marx
The quartet practiced in the park
And we sang dirges in the dark
The day the music died.
We were singin':

Chorus

Verse 4
Helter-skelter in the summer swelter,
The birds flew off to a fallout shelter.
Eight miles high and fallin' fast,
It landed foul on the grass.
The players tried for a forward pass,
With the jester on the sidelines in a cast.
Now that halftime air was sweet perfume,
While the sergeants played a marching tune.
We all got up to dance,
But we never got the chance,
'Cause the players tried to take the field,
The marching band refused to yield,
Do you recall what was revealed,
The day the music died.
We started singin':

Chorus

Verse 5
And there we were all in one place,
A generation lost in space,
With no time left to start again.
So come on, Jack be nimble, Jack be quick,
Jack Flash sat on a candlestick.
'Cause fire is the devil's only friend.
And as I watched him on the stage
My hands were clenched in fists of rage.
No angel born in hell,
Could break that Satan's spell
And as the flames climbed high into the night
To light the sacrificial rite
I saw Satan laughing with delight
The day the music died.
He was singin':

Chorus

Verse 6 *(chords as intro)*
I met a girl who sang the blues,
And I asked her for some happy news,
But she just smiled and turned away.
I went down to the sacred store,
Where I heard the music years before,
But the man there said the music wouldn't play.
And in the streets the children screamed,
The lovers cried and the poets dreamed.
Not a word was spoken,
The church bells all were broken.
And the three men I admire most,
The Father, Son and the Holy Ghost
They caught the last train for the coast,
The day the music died.
And they were singin':

⊕ *Coda*

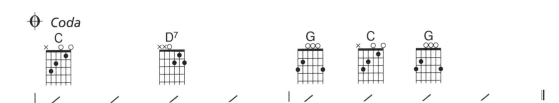

Brown Eyed Girl

Words & Music by Van Morrison

Verse

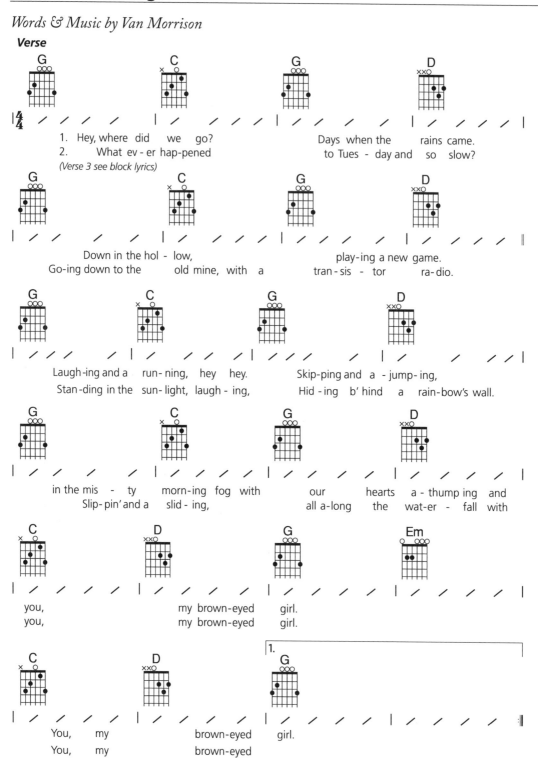

1. Hey, where did we go?   Days when the rains came.
2. What ev - er hap-pened   to Tues - day and so slow?

(Verse 3 see block lyrics)

Down in the hol - low,   play-ing a new game.
Go-ing down to the old mine, with a   tran - sis - tor ra - dio.

Laugh-ing and a run - ning, hey hey.   Skip-ping and a - jump-ing,
Stan-ding in the sun - light, laugh - ing,   Hid - ing b' hind a rain-bow's wall.

in the mis - ty morn-ing fog with   our hearts a - thump ing and
Slip- pin' and a slid - ing,   all a-long the wat-er - fall with

you,   my brown-eyed girl.
you,   my brown-eyed girl.

1.

You, my   brown-eyed girl.
You, my   brown-eyed

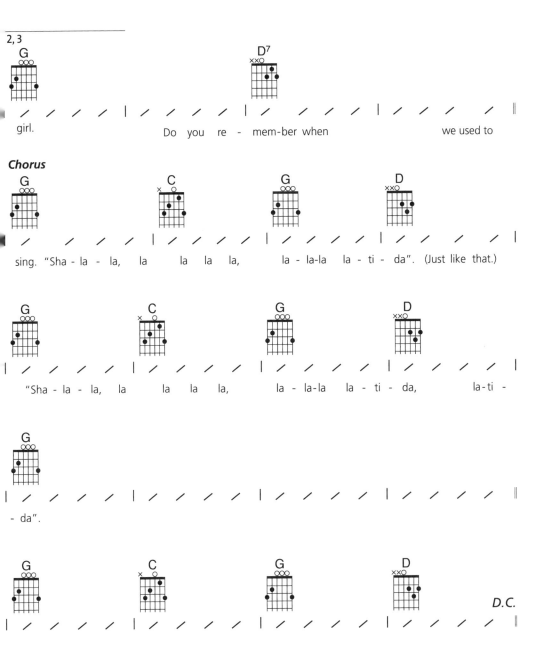

2, 3

girl.   Do you re - mem-ber when   we used to

Chorus

sing. "Sha - la - la,   la   la   la   la,   la - la-la   la - ti - da". (Just like that.)

"Sha - la - la,   la   la   la   la,   la - la-la   la - ti - da,   la- ti -

- da".

D.C.

Verse 3
So hard to find my way, now that I'm all on my own.
I saw you just the other day, my how you have grown.
Cast my memory back there, Lord, sometimes I'm overcome just thinking about it.
Laughing and a-running, hey hey, behind the stadium with you,
My brown-eyed girl
You, my brown-eyed girl.
Do you remember when we used to sing.

Chorus
(Repeat to fade)

God Only Knows

Words & Music by Brian Wilson & Tony Asher

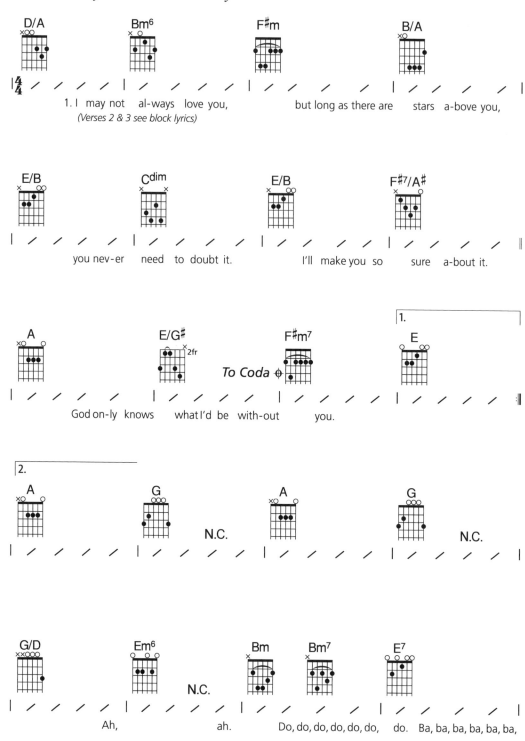

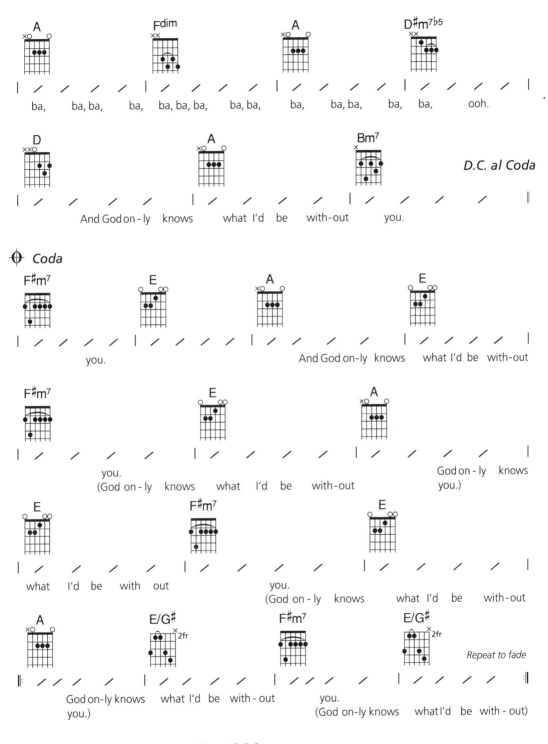

| A | | Fdim | | A | | D#m7b5 | |
| ba, | ba, ba, | ba, | ba, ba, ba, | ba, ba, | ba, | ba, ba, | ba, ba, | ooh. |

| D | | A | | Bm7 | | *D.C. al Coda* |
| And God on-ly knows | what I'd be | with-out | you. |

⊕ Coda

| F#m7 | | E | | A | | E | |
| you. | | | And God on-ly knows | what I'd be with-out |

F#m7		E		A	
you.	God on-ly knows
(God on-ly knows what I'd be with-out	you.)

| E | | F#m7 | | E | |
| what I'd be with out | you. |
| (God on-ly knows what I'd be with-out |

A		E/G# 2fr		F#m7		E/G# 2fr	
						Repeat to fade
God on-ly knows what I'd be with-out	you.
you.)	(God on-ly knows what I'd be with-out)

Verses 2 & 3
If you should ever leave me,
Though life would still go on, believe me,
The world could show nothing to me,
So what good would living do me?
God only knows what I'd be without you.

13

Grace Kelly

Words & Music by Jodi Marr, Dan Warner, Mika & John Merchant

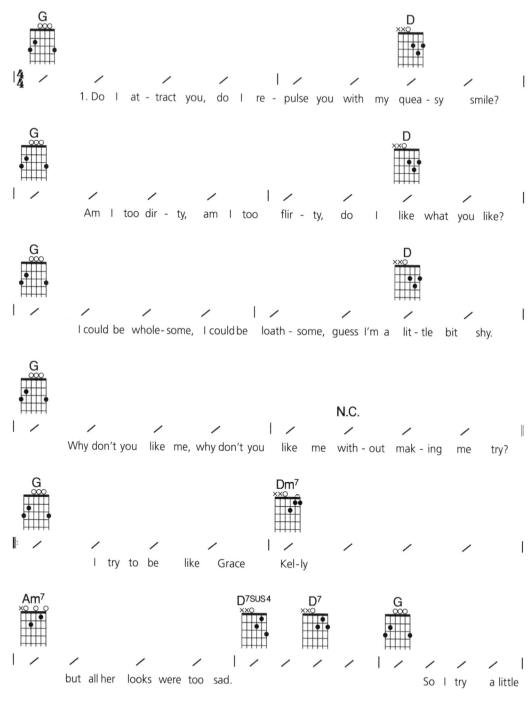

G   D

1. Do I at - tract you, do I re - pulse you with my quea - sy smile?

G   D

Am I too dir - ty, am I too flir - ty, do I like what you like?

G   D

I could be whole-some, I could be loath - some, guess I'm a lit - tle bit shy.

G   N.C.

Why don't you like me, why don't you like me with - out mak - ing me try?

G   Dm⁷

I try to be like Grace Kel-ly

Am⁷   D⁷SUS4   D⁷   G

but all her looks were too sad. So I try a little

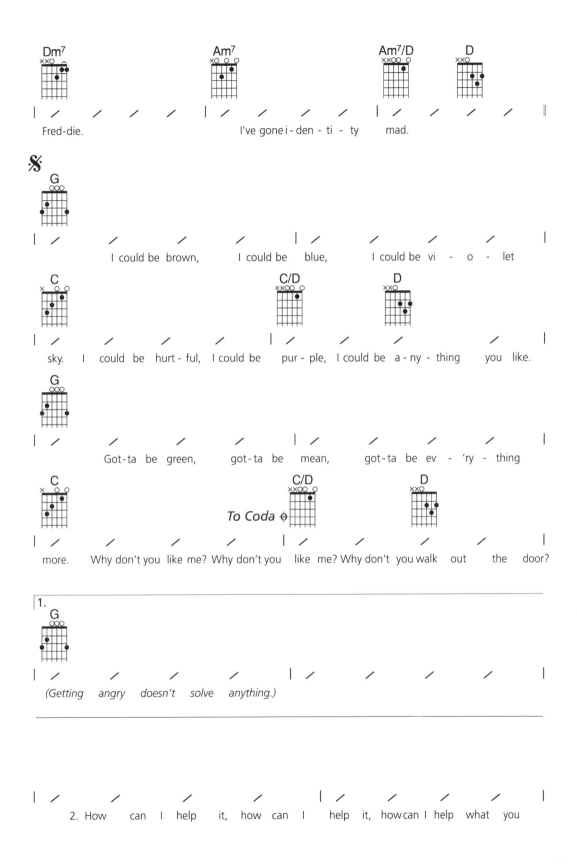

Dm⁷ / / / / **Am⁷** / / / / **Am⁷/D** / / / / **D**

Fred-die.   I've gone i - den - ti - ty   mad.

𝄋

G / / / / / / / / /

I could be brown,   I could be   blue,   I could be vi - o - let

C / / / / **C/D** / / **D** /

sky. I could be hurt - ful, I could be   pur - ple, I could be a - ny - thing   you like.

G / / / / / / / / /

Got-ta be green,   got-ta be   mean,   got-ta be ev - 'ry - thing

C / / / / **C/D** / / **D** /

To Coda ⊕

more.   Why don't you like me? Why don't you   like me? Why don't you walk   out   the   door?

1.
G / / / / / / / /

(Getting   angry   doesn't   solve   anything.)

/ / / / / / / /

2. How   can I help   it, how can I   help   it, howcan I help what you

15

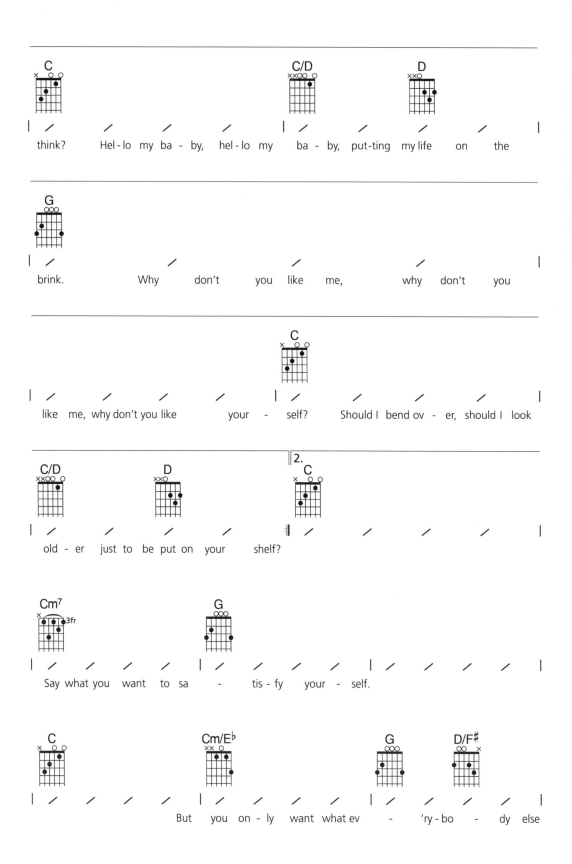

C

think? Hel-lo my ba - by, hel-lo my ba - by, put-ting my life on the

G

brink. Why don't you like me, why don't you

C

like me, why don't you like your - self? Should I bend ov - er, should I look

C/D **D** **‖2.** **C**

old - er just to be put on your shelf?

Cm⁷ **G**

Say what you want to sa - tis-fy your - self.

C **Cm/E♭** **G** **D/F♯**

But you on - ly want what ev - 'ry - bo - dy else

16

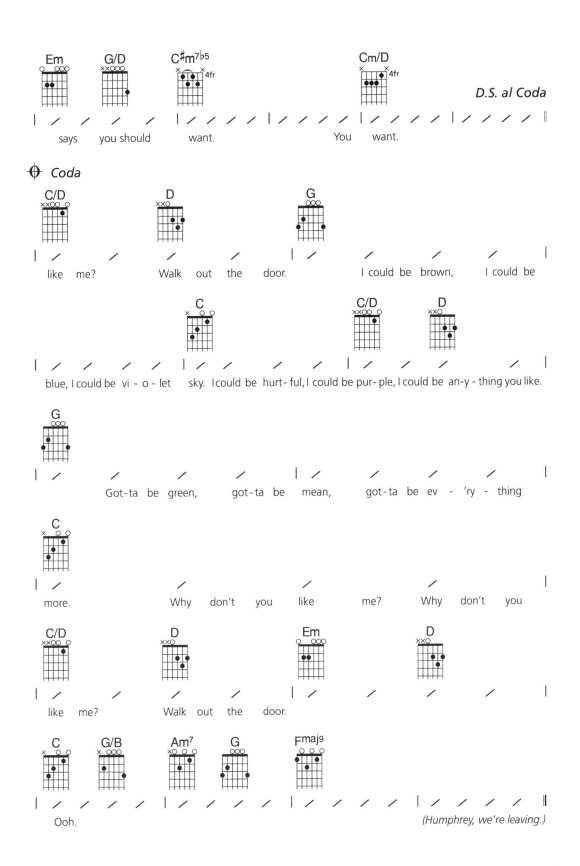

Em **G/D** **C#m7b5**   **Cm/D**

D.S. al Coda

| / / / / | / / / / | / / / / | / / / / | / / / / ‖

says   you should   want.   You   want.

⊕ *Coda*

C/D   **D**   **G**

| / / / | / / / |

like   me?   Walk out the   door.   I could be brown,   I could be

C   **C/D** **D**

| / / / / | / / / / | / / / / |

blue, I could be vi - o - let sky. I could be hurt- ful, I could be pur- ple, I could be an-y - thing you like.

G

| / / / / | / / / / |

Got-ta be green,   got-ta be   mean,   got-ta be ev – 'ry – thing

C

| / / / | / |

more.   Why don't you   like   me?   Why   don't   you

C/D **D**   **Em**   **D**

| / / / / | / / / / |

like   me?   Walk out the   door.

C **G/B** **Am7** **G** **Fmaj9**

| / / / / | / / / / | / / / / | / / / / ‖

Ooh.   *(Humphrey, we're leaving.)*

17

Don't Think Twice, It's All Right

Words & Music by Bob Dylan

(To match original recording, use a capo 4th fret)

C

1. It ain't no use to sit and won-der why, babe,
(Verses 2-5 see block lyrics)

Am/G **F**

it don't mat-ter, an-y how.

C **G** **C**

An' it ain't no use to

G **Am** **Am/G**

sit and won-der why, babe,

D⁷/F♯ **G**

if you don't know by now.

G⁷ **C**

When your roost-er crows at the break

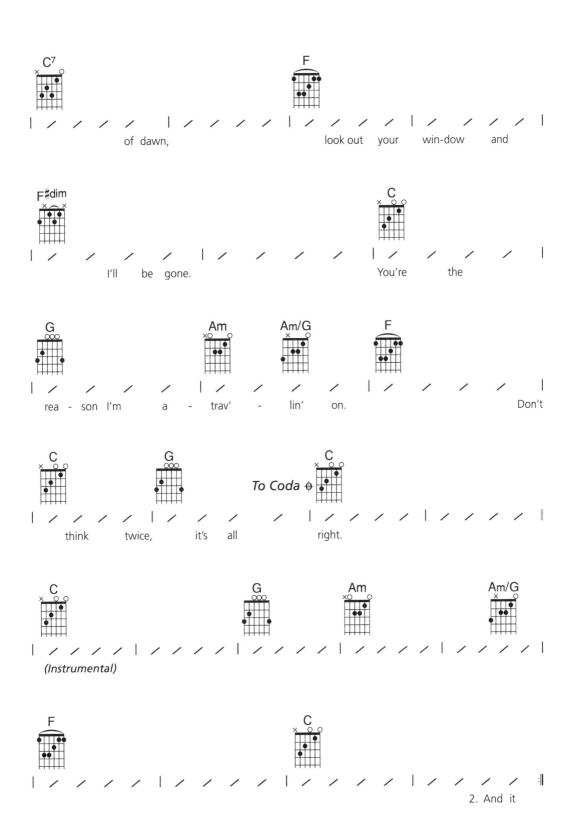

of dawn,   look out   your   win-dow   and

I'll   be   gone.   You're   the

rea - son I'm   a   -   trav'   -   lin'   on.   Don't

think   twice,   it's   all   right.

To Coda

(Instrumental)

2. And it

Verse 2

It ain't no use in turnin' on your light, babe
That light I never knowed
An' it ain't no use in turnin' on your light, babe
I'm on the dark side of the road
Still I wish there was somethin' you would do or say
To try and make me change my mind and stay
We never did too much talkin' anyway
So don't think twice, it's all right.

Verse 3

It ain't no use in callin' out my name, gal
Like you never did before
It ain't no use in callin' out my name, gal
I can't hear you anymore
I'm a-thinkin' and a-wond'rin' all the way down the road
I once loved a woman, a child I'm told
I give her my heart but she wanted my soul
But don't think twice, it's all right.

Verse 4

I'm walkin' down that long, lonesome road, babe
Where I'm bound, I can't tell
But goodbye's too good a word, gal
So I'll just say fare thee well
I ain't sayin' you treated me unkind
You could have done better but I don't mind
You just kinda wasted my precious time
But don't think twice, it's all right.

Verse 5

(Instrumental to Coda)

Ⓓ **Coda**

C   F   C

20

Heaven Knows I'm Miserable Now

Words & Music by Morrissey & Johnny Marr

(To match original recording, use a capo 2nd fret)

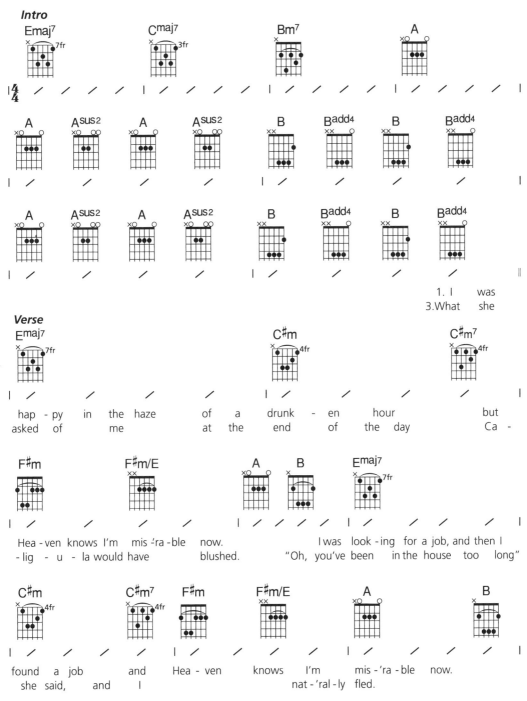

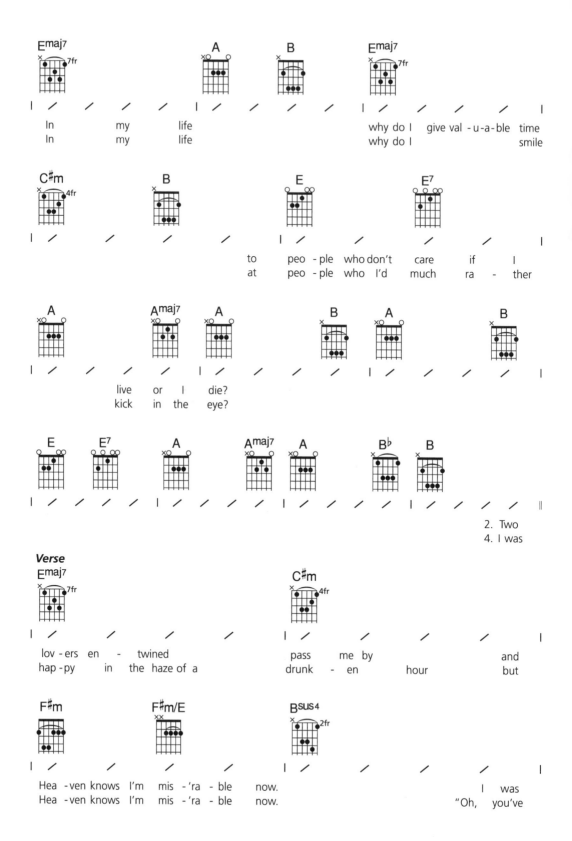

In my life   why do I give val - u - a - ble time

In my life   why do I   smile

to   peo - ple who don't care   if   I

at   peo - ple who I'd much ra - ther

live or I die?

kick in the eye?

2. Two

4. I was

Verse

lov - ers en - twined   pass me by   and

hap - py in the haze of a   drunk - en   hour   but

Hea - ven knows I'm mis - 'ra - ble now.

Hea - ven knows I'm mis - 'ra - ble now.

I was

"Oh, you've

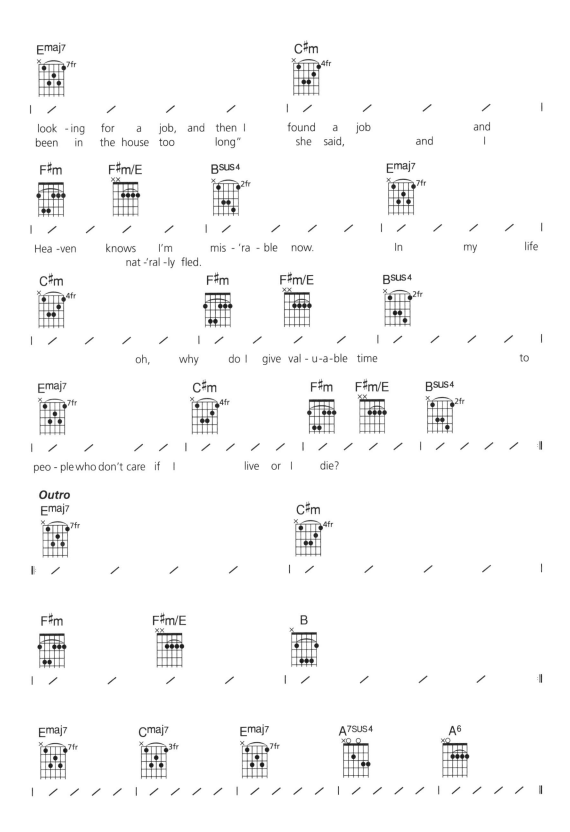

Emaj7   C#m

look - ing   for   a   job,   and   then I   found   a   job   and
been   in   the   house   too   long"   she   said,   and   I

F#m   F#m/E   Bsus4   Emaj7

Hea -ven   knows   I'm   mis - 'ra - ble   now.   In   my   life
           nat -'ral -ly fled.

C#m   F#m   F#m/E   Bsus4

       oh,   why   do I   give val - u-a-ble time   to

Emaj7   C#m   F#m   F#m/E   Bsus4

peo - ple who don't care   if   I   live   or I   die?

Outro

Emaj7   C#m

F#m   F#m/E   B

Emaj7   Cmaj7   Emaj7   A7sus4   A6

If You Could Read My Mind

Words & Music by Gordon Lightfoot

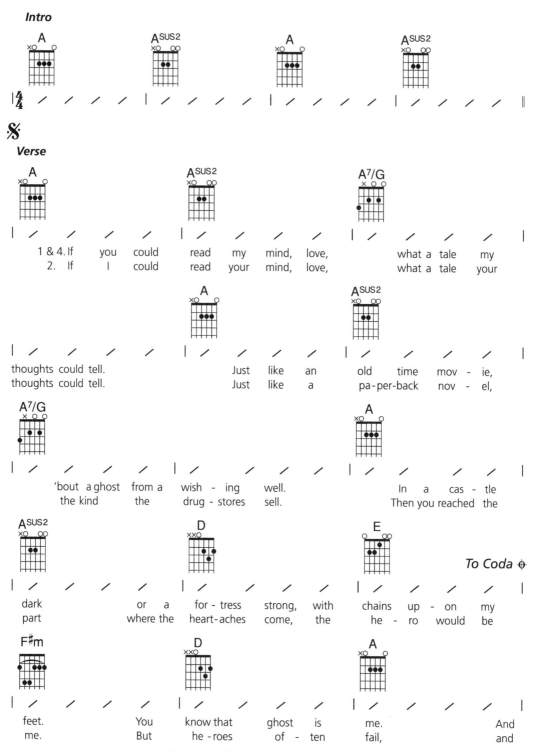

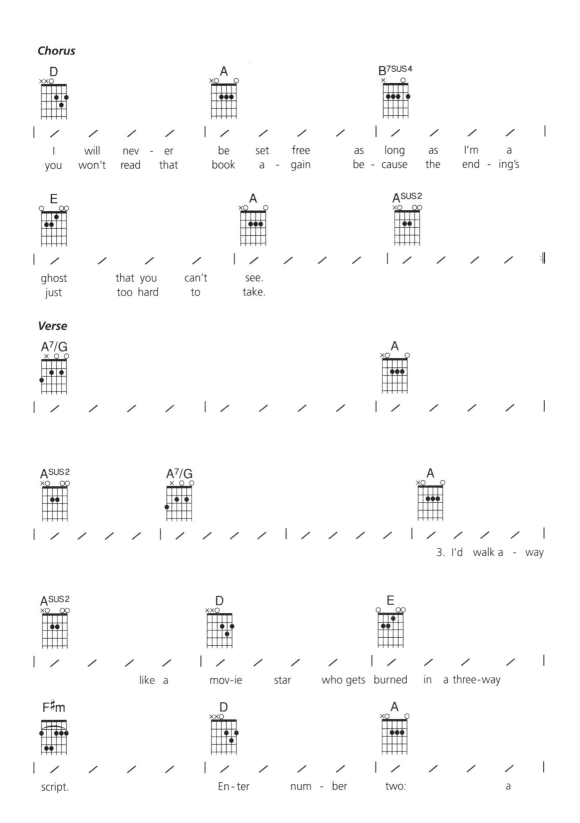

Chorus

D   A   B⁷ˢᵘˢ⁴

| / / / | / / / | / / / |

I will nev - er be set free as long as I'm a
you won't read that book a - gain be - cause the end - ing's

E   A   Aˢᵘˢ²

| / / / | / / / | / / / :‖

ghost that you can't see.
just too hard to take.

Verse

A⁷/G   A

| / / / | / / / | / / / |

Aˢᵘˢ²   A⁷/G   A

| / / / | / / / | / / / |

3. I'd walk a - way

Aˢᵘˢ²   D   E

| / / / | / / / | / / / |

like a mov-ie star who gets burned in a three-way

F♯m   D   A

| / / / | / / / | / / / |

script. En - ter num - ber two: a

Chorus

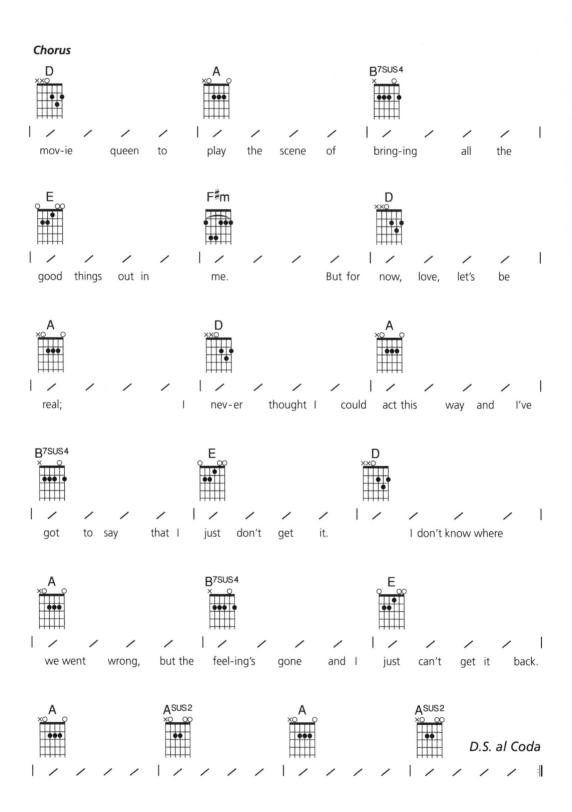

D	A	B7SUS4
mov-ie queen to	play the scene of	bring-ing all the

E	F#m	D
good things out in	me.	But for now, love, let's be

A	D	A
real;	I nev-er thought I	could act this way and I've

B7SUS4	E	D
got to say that I	just don't get it.	I don't know where

A	B7SUS4	E
we went wrong, but the	feel-ing's gone and I	just can't get it back.

A	ASUS2	A	ASUS2
			D.S. al Coda

26

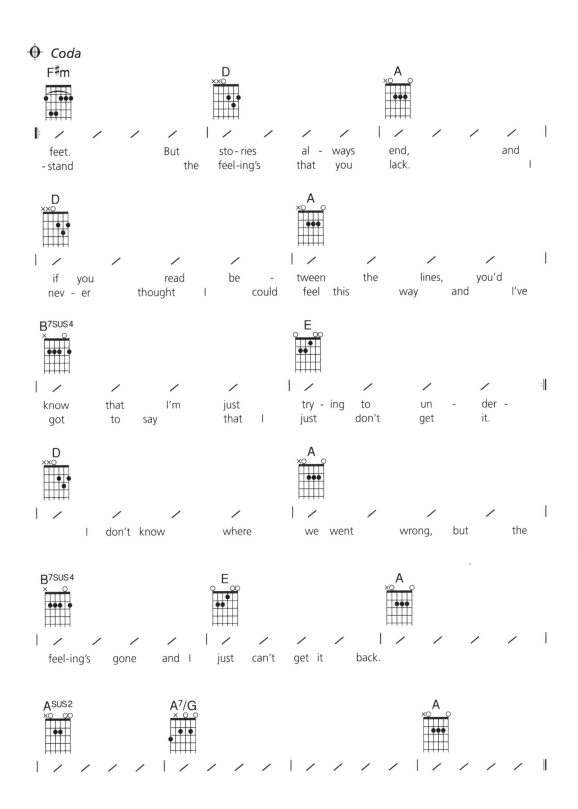

$\oplus$ *Coda*

F#m

/ / / / | / / / / | / / / / |

feet. But sto - ries al - ways end, and
- stand the feel-ing's that you lack.

D **A**

/ / / / | / / / / |

if you read be - tween the lines, you'd
nev - er thought I could feel this way and I've

B7SUS4 **E**

/ / / / | / / / / |

know that I'm just try - ing to un - der -
got to say that I just don't get it.

D **A**

/ / / / | / / / / |

I don't know where we went wrong, but the

B7SUS4 **E** **A**

/ / / / | / / / / | / / / / |

feel-ing's gone and I just can't get it back.

ASUS2 **A7/G** **A**

/ / / / | / / / / | / / / / | / / / / ‖

I Walk The Line

Words & Music by Johnny Cash

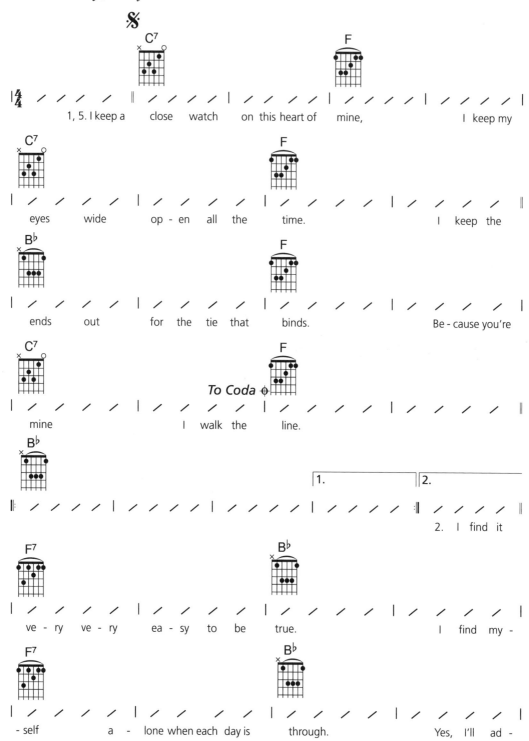

1, 5. I keep a close watch on this heart of mine, I keep my eyes wide op - en all the time. I keep the ends out for the tie that binds. Be - cause you're mine I walk the line.

2. I find it ve - ry ve - ry ea - sy to be true. I find my - self a - lone when each day is through. Yes, I'll ad -

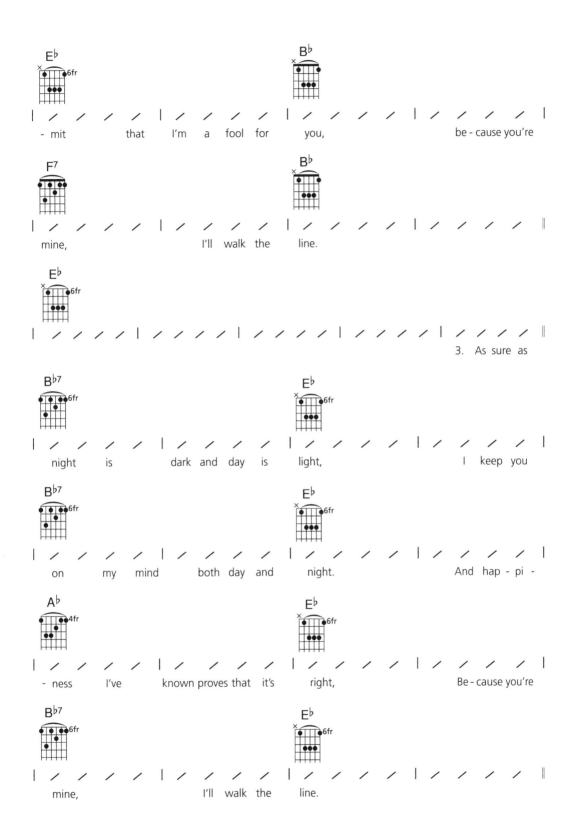

E♭

B♭

| / / / / | / / / / | / / / / | / / / / |
\- mit   that   I'm a fool for you,   be - cause you're

F⁷

B♭

| / / / / | / / / / | / / / / | / / / / ‖
mine,   I'll walk the   line.

E♭

| / / / / | / / / / | / / / / | / / / / | / / / / ‖
                                              3. As sure as

B♭⁷

E♭

| / / / / | / / / / | / / / / | / / / / |
night   is   dark and day is   light,   I keep you

B♭⁷

E♭

| / / / / | / / / / | / / / / | / / / / |
on   my mind both day and night.   And hap - pi -

A♭

E♭

| / / / / | / / / / | / / / / | / / / / |
\- ness I've   known proves that it's   right,   Be - cause you're

B♭⁷

E♭

| / / / / | / / / / | / / / / | / / / / ‖
mine,   I'll walk the   line.

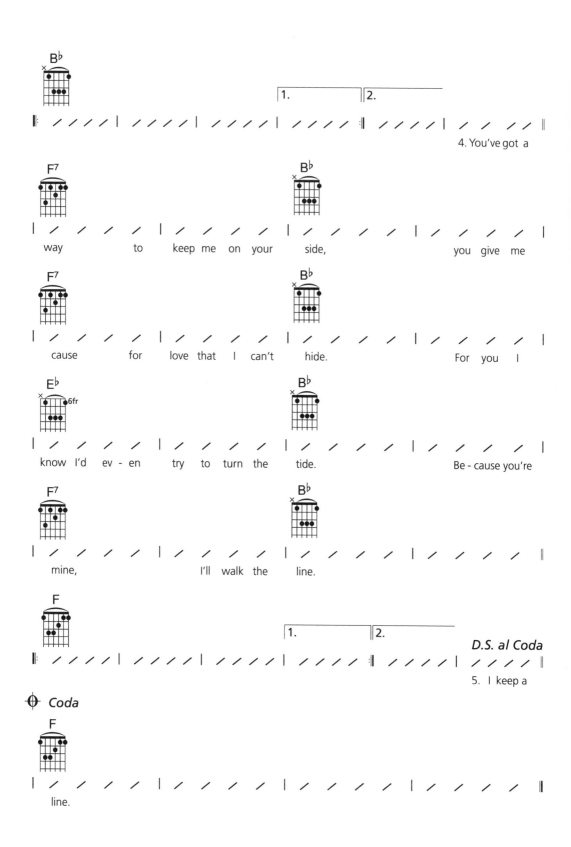

Bb

1.   2.

4. You've got a

F7   Bb

way   to   keep me on your   side,   you give me

F7   Bb

cause   for   love that I can't   hide.   For you I

Eb   Bb
6fr

know I'd ev - en   try   to turn the   tide.   Be - cause you're

F7   Bb

mine,   I'll walk the   line.

F

1.   2.

D.S. al Coda

5. I keep a

Coda

F

line.

30

In The Summertime

Words & Music by Ray Dorset

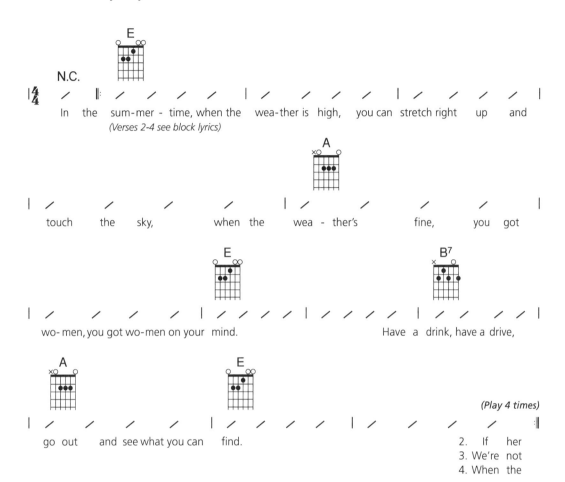

In the sum-mer - time, when the wea-ther is high, you can stretch right up and
(Verses 2-4 see block lyrics)

touch the sky, when the wea - ther's fine, you got

wo- men, you got wo-men on your mind. Have a drink, have a drive,

(Play 4 times)

go out and see what you can find.

2. If her
3. We're not
4. When the

Verse 2
If her daddy's rich take her out for a meal;
If her daddy's poor just do as you feel.
Speed along the lane, do a ton, or a ton and twenty-five.
When the sun goes down you can make it, make it good in a lay-by.

Verse 3
We're not grey people, we're not dirty, we're not mean,
We love everybody but we do as we please.
When the weather's fine we go fishing, or go swimming in the sea.
We're always happy, life's for living, yeah! That's our philosophy.

Verse 4
When the winter's here, yeah! It's party time;
Bring a bottle, wear your bright clothes, it'll soon be summertime.
And we'll sing again, we'll go driving or maybe we'll settle down.
If she's rich, if she's nice, bring your friends and we'll all go into town.

More Than A Feeling

Words & Music by Tom Scholz

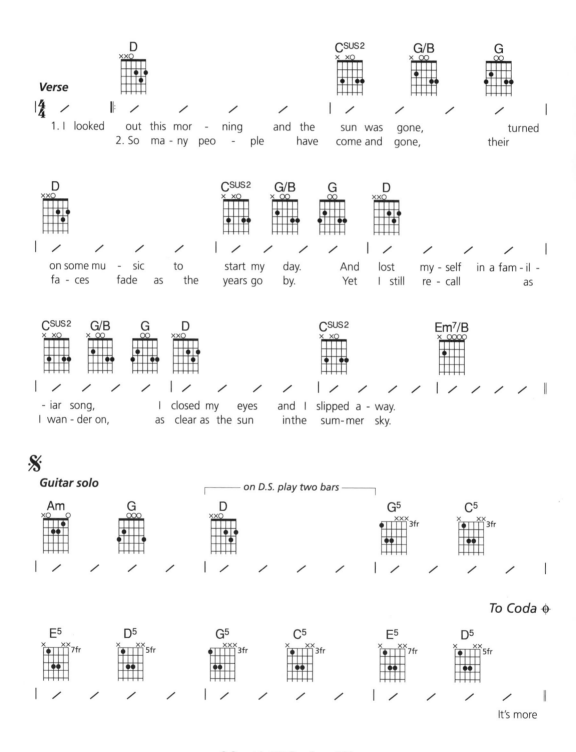

1. I looked out this mor - ning and the sun was gone, turned
2. So ma - ny peo - ple have come and gone, their

on some mu - sic to start my day. And lost my - self in a fam - il -
fa - ces fade as the years go by. Yet I still re - call as

- iar song, I closed my eyes and I slipped a - way.
I wan - der on, as clear as the sun in the sum - mer sky.

Guitar solo

— on D.S. play two bars —

To Coda

It's more

Chorus

G5   C5   E5   D5   G5   C5

| / / / / | / / / / | / / / / |

than a feel - ing,   when I   hear   that old   song   they used

E5   D5   G5   C5   E5   D5

| / / / / | / / / / | / / / / |

to   play.   I be - gin dream - ing,   till   I

G5   C5   Eb   Em7

| / / / / | / / / / | / / / / |

see Mar - i - anne   walk   a - way.   I see my   Mar-

A   **1.**   G   D/F#   Em

| / / / / | / / / / | / / / / |

- i - anne   walk - ing   a - way.

D   Csus2   G/B   G   D   Csus2   G/B   G

| / / / / | / / / / | / / / / | / / / / :||

2.

Bm   Bm/A   G   D/F#   Asus4   A

| / / / / | / / / / | / / / / | / / / / ||

33

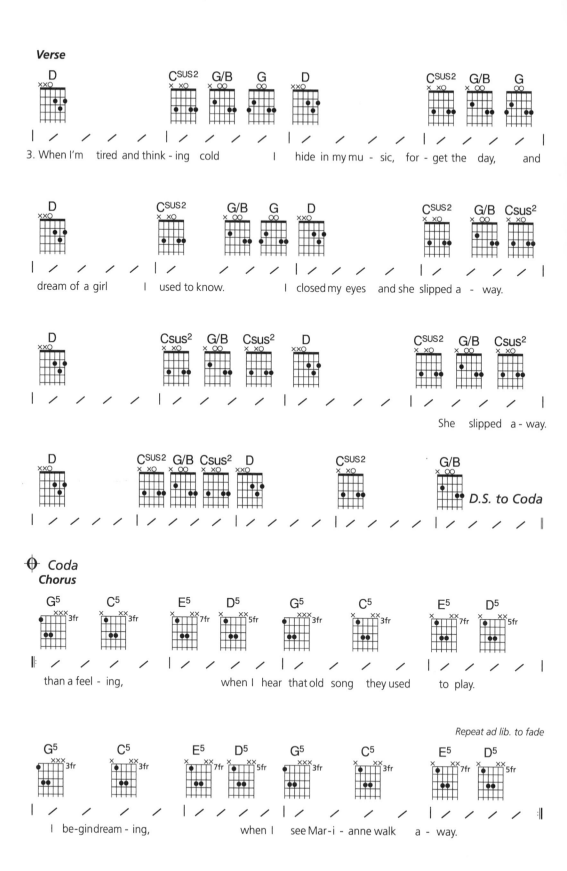

Verse

3. When I'm tired and think - ing cold | hide in my mu - sic, for - get the day, and

dream of a girl | used to know. | closed my eyes and she slipped a - way.

She slipped a - way.

D.S. to Coda

Coda
Chorus

than a feel - ing, when I hear that old song they used to play.

Repeat ad lib. to fade

I be-gin dream - ing, when I see Mar-i - anne walk a - way.

Naïve

Words & Music by Luke Pritchard, Hugh Harris, Max Rafferty & Paul Garred

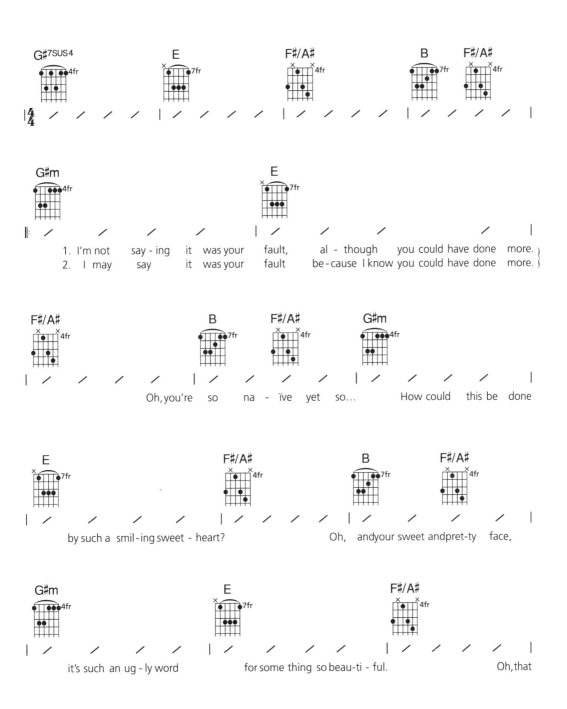

1. I'm not say-ing it was your fault, al-though you could have done more.
2. I may say it was your fault be-cause I know you could have done more.

Oh, you're so na-ïve yet so... How could this be done

by such a smil-ing sweet-heart? Oh, and your sweet and pret-ty face,

it's such an ug-ly word for some thing so beau-ti-ful. Oh, that

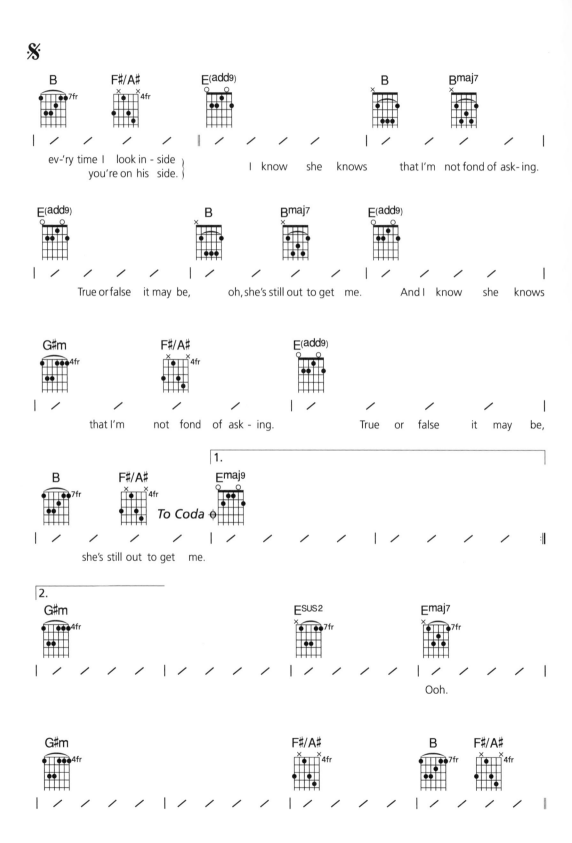

%

| B | F#/A# | E(add9) | | B | Bmaj7 |

ev-'ry time I look in - side
you're on his side.

I know she knows that I'm not fond of ask- ing.

| E(add9) | | B | Bmaj7 | E(add9) |

True or false it may be, oh, she's still out to get me. And I know she knows

| G#m | F#/A# | E(add9) |

that I'm not fond of ask - ing. True or false it may be,

1.

| B | F#/A# | Emaj9 |

To Coda ⊕

she's still out to get me.

2.

| G#m | | Esus2 | Emaj7 |

Ooh.

| G#m | | F#/A# | B | F#/A# |

36

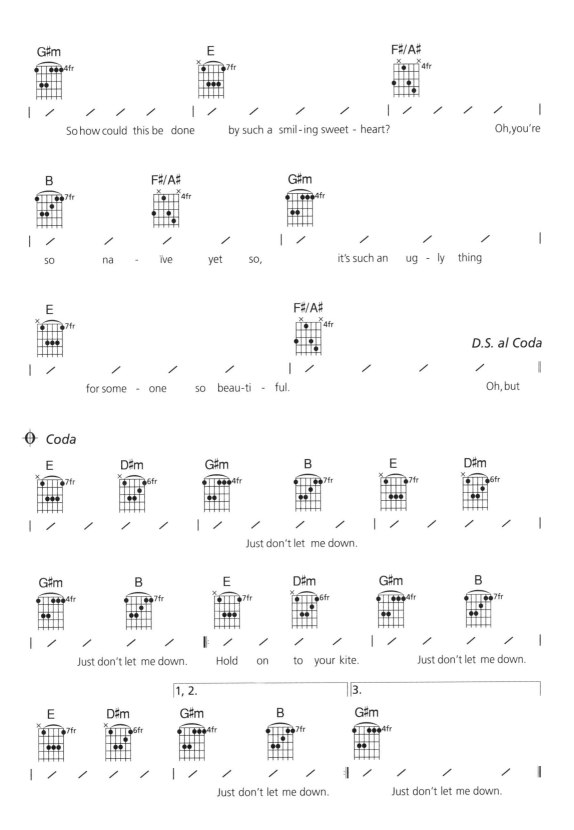

So how could this be done   by such a smil-ing sweet-heart?   Oh, you're

so   na - ïve   yet   so,   it's such an   ug - ly   thing

for some - one   so   beau-ti - ful.   Oh, but

D.S. al Coda

✛ *Coda*

Just don't let me down.

Just don't let me down.   Hold   on   to   your kite.   Just don't let me down.

1, 2.   **3.**

Just don't let me down.   Just don't let me down.

37

Redemption Song

Words & Music by Bob Marley

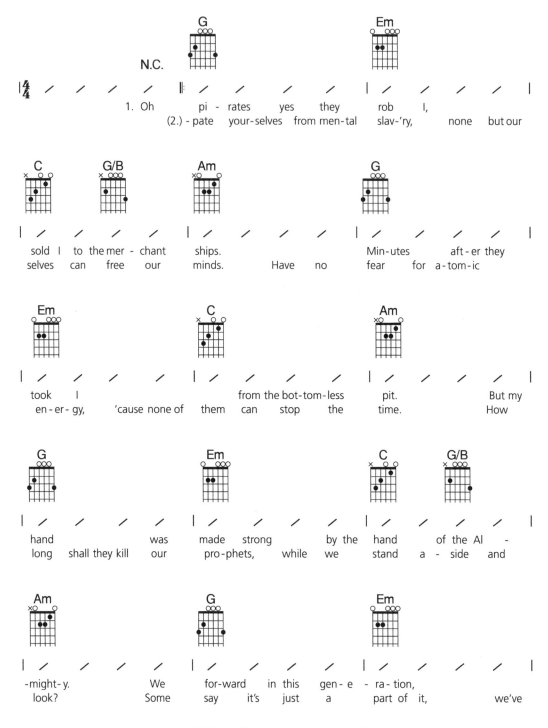

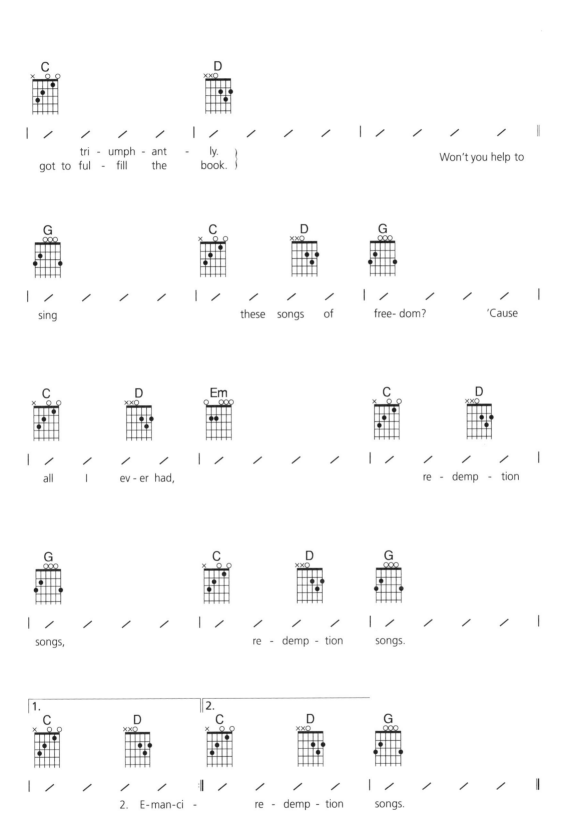

Sweet Home Alabama

Words & Music by Ronnie Van Zant, Ed King & Gary Rossington

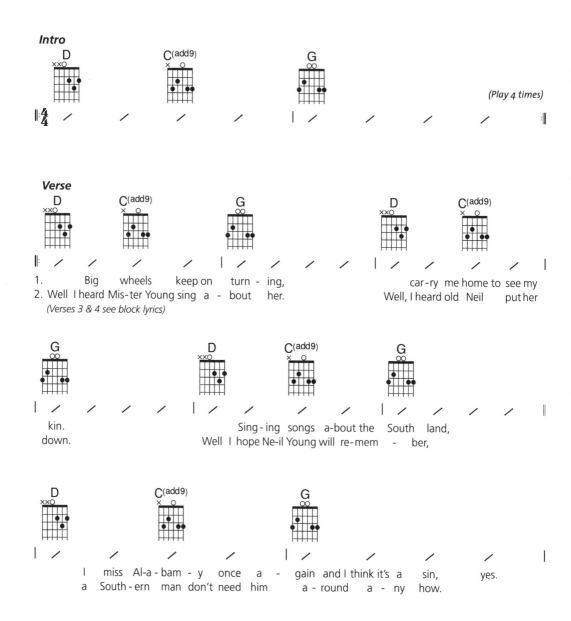

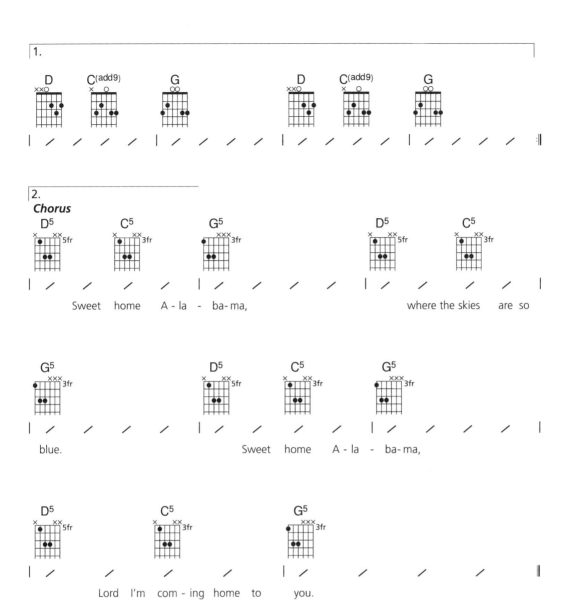

1.

D   C(add9)   G   D   C(add9)   G

2.

Chorus

D5   C5   G5   D5   C5

Sweet   home   A - la   -   ba- ma,   where the skies   are so

G5   D5   C5   G5

blue.   Sweet   home   A - la   -   ba- ma,

D5   C5   G5

Lord   I'm   com - ing home to   you.

Verse 3
In Birmingham they love the gov'nor, boo, hoo, hoo.
Now we all did what we could do.
Now Watergate does not bother me,
Does your conscience bother you? (Tell the truth)

Chorus

Verse 4
Now Muscle Shoals has got the swampers,
And they've been known to pick a song or two.
Lord they get me off so much
They pick me up when I'm feeling blue.
Now how 'bout you?

Chorus

The Tide Is High

Words & Music by John Holt, Howard Barrett & Tyrone Evans

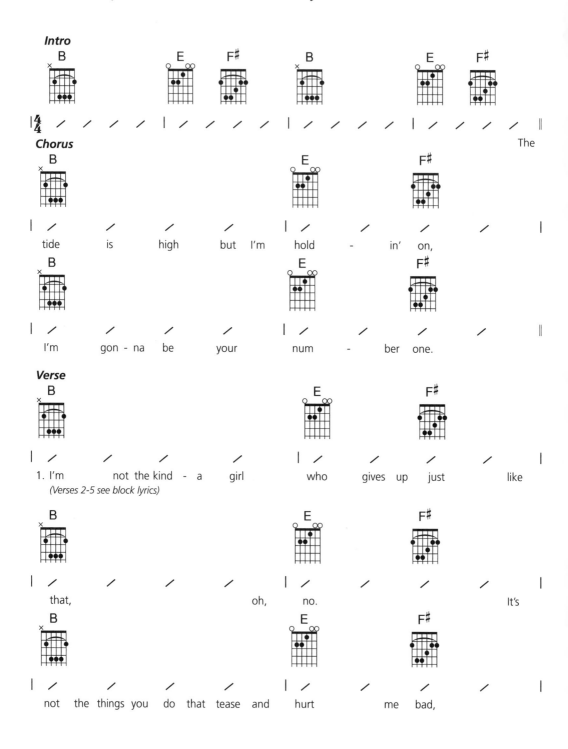

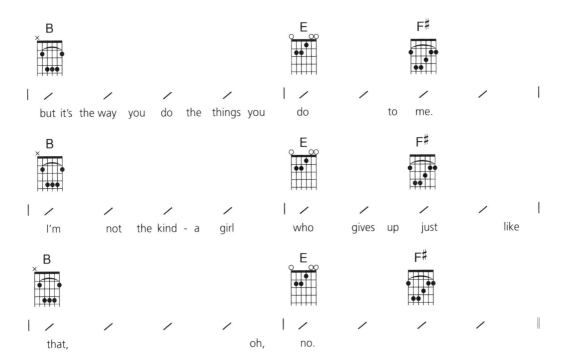

B				E		F#			
but it's	the way	you	do	the	things you	do		to	me.

B				E		F#			
I'm	not	the kind - a	girl		who	gives	up	just	like

B				E		F#			
that,					oh,	no.			

Chorus

Verse 2
I'm not the kind-a girl who gives up just like that, oh, no.
It's not the things you do that tease and hurt me bad,
But it's the way you do the things you do to me.
I'm not the kind-a girl who gives up just like that, oh, no.

Chorus

Verse 3
I'm not the kind-a girl who gives up just like that, oh, no.
Ev'ry girl wants you to be her man,
But I'll wait, my dear, till it's my turn.
I'm not the kind-a girl who gives up just like that, oh, no.

Chorus

Verse 4
(Instrumental)

Chorus

Verse 3
I'm not the kind-a girl who gives up just like that, oh, no.
Ev'ry girl wants you to be her man,
But I'll wait, my dear, till it's my turn.
I'm not the kind-a girl who gives up just like that, oh, no.

Chorus
(Repeat to fade)

Yellow

Words & Music by Guy Berryman, Chris Martin, Jon Buckland & Will Champion

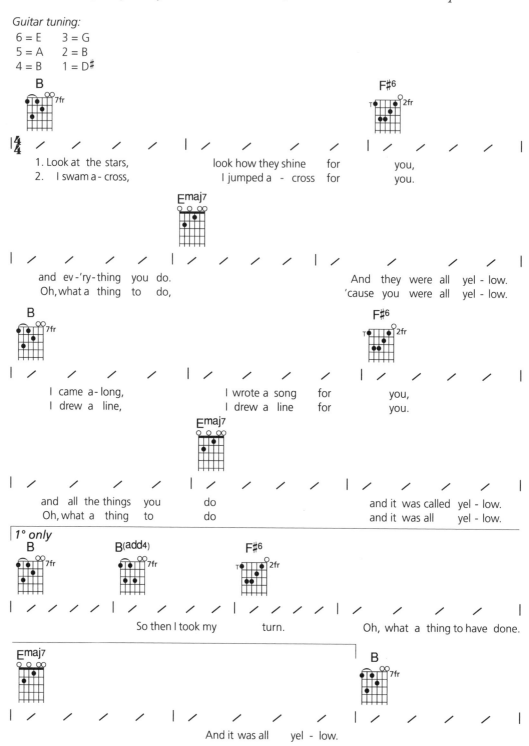

Guitar tuning:
6 = E   3 = G
5 = A   2 = B
4 = B   1 = D#

1. Look at the stars, look how they shine for you,
2. I swam a-cross, I jumped a - cross for you.

and ev-'ry-thing you do. And they were all yel - low.
Oh, what a thing to do, 'cause you were all yel - low.

I came a-long, I wrote a song for you,
I drew a line, I drew a line for you.

and all the things you do and it was called yel - low.
Oh, what a thing to do and it was all yel - low.

1° only

So then I took my turn. Oh, what a thing to have done.

And it was all yel - low.

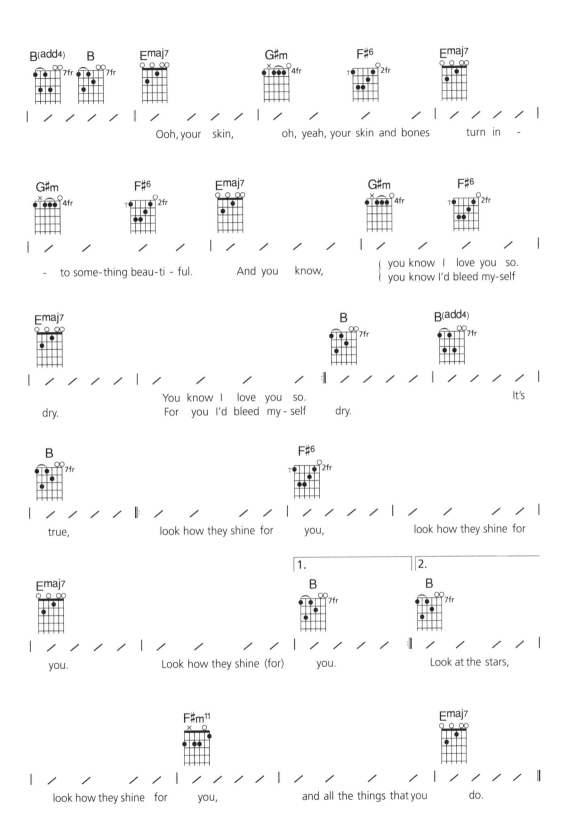

You Shook Me All Night Long

Words & Music by Angus Young, Malcolm Young & Brian Johnson

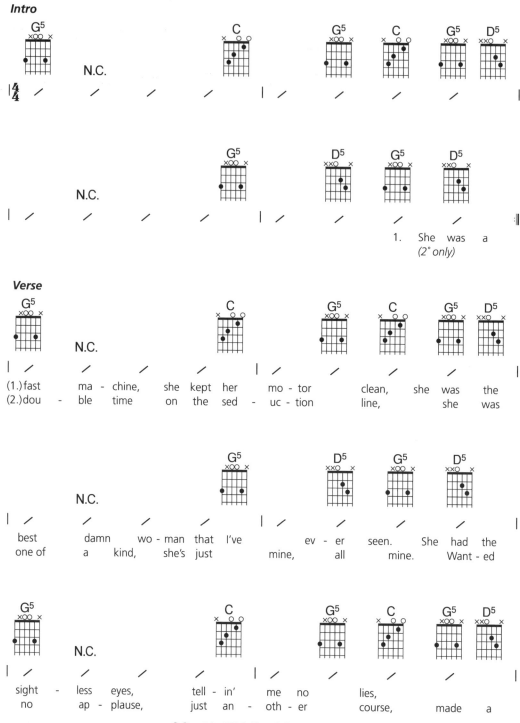

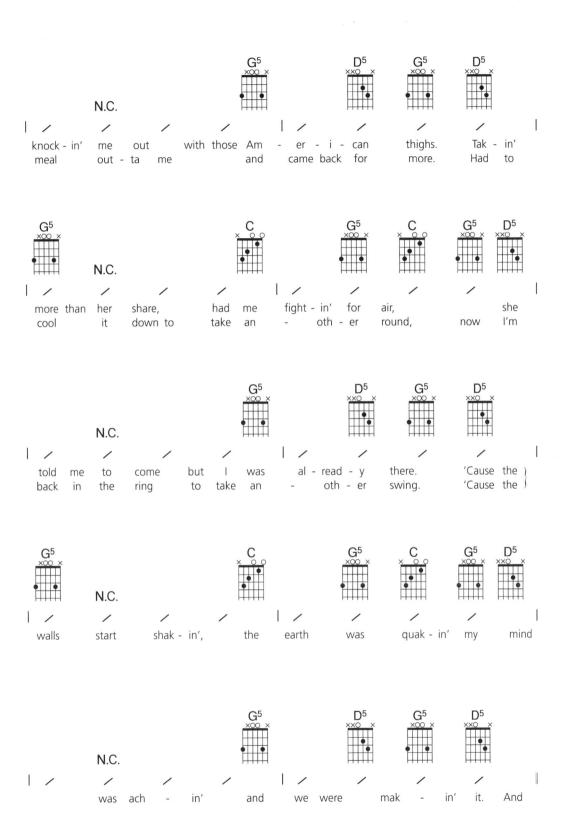

Line 1 (N.C. | G5 | D5 G5 D5 |):
knock - in' me out with those Am - er - i - can thighs. Tak - in'
meal out - ta me and came back for more. Had to

Line 2 (G5 N.C. | C | G5 C G5 D5 |):
more than her share, had me fight - in' for air, she
cool it down to take an - oth - er round, now I'm

Line 3 (N.C. | G5 | D5 G5 D5 |):
told me to come but I was al - read - y there. 'Cause the
back in the ring to take an - oth - er swing. 'Cause the

Line 4 (G5 N.C. | C | G5 C G5 D5 |):
walls start shak - in', the earth was quak - in' my mind

Line 5 (N.C. | G5 | D5 G5 D5 |):
was ach - in' and we were mak - in' it. And

47

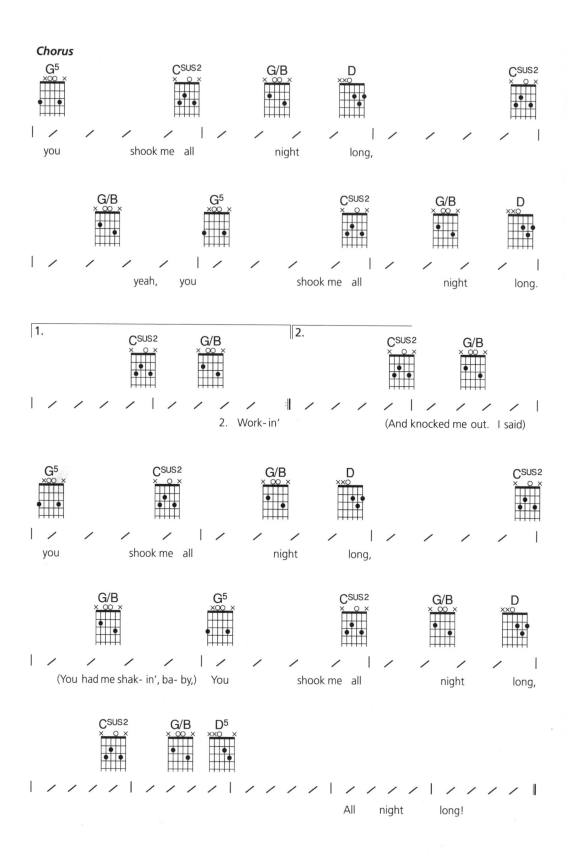

Chorus

you shook me all night long,

yeah, you shook me all night long.

1.
2. Work-in'

2. (And knocked me out. I said)

you shook me all night long,

(You had me shak-in', ba-by,) You shook me all night long,

All night long!

1 2 3 4 5 6 7 8 9